I SPY

A PUMPKIN

For Ian Michael Grant McPherson Ortiz—Welcome!
—J.M.

For Max Mindich
—W.W.

Text copyright © 2005 by Jean Marzollo.
"Toy Planet" from *I Spy Fantasy* © 1994 by Walter Wick; "A Secret Cupboard," "Good Morning," and "House on the Hill" from *I Spy Spooky Night* © 1996 by Walter Wick; "Arts & Crafts," "Toys in the Attic," and "Silhouettes" from *I Spy* © 1992 by Walter Wick; "Levers, Ramps, and Pulleys" and "Patterns and Paint" from *I Spy School Days* © 1995 by Walter Wick.

Library of Congress Cataloging-in-Publication Data is available.

ISBN-13: 978-0-439-73863-7
ISBN-10: 0-439-73863-6

56 55 54 53

23/0

Printed in the U.S.A. 40 • This edition first printing, June 2008

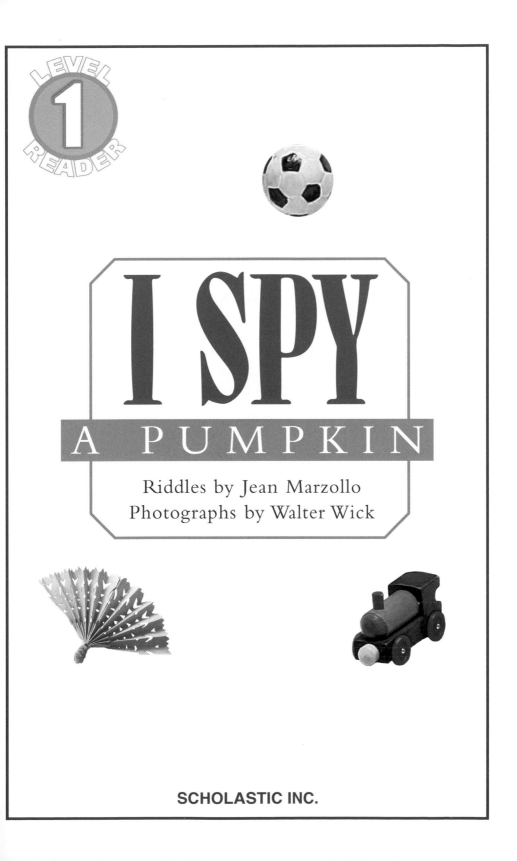

I SPY
A PUMPKIN

Riddles by Jean Marzollo
Photographs by Walter Wick

SCHOLASTIC INC.

I spy

 a pumpkin,

a bushy hare,

 a skull,

 a wagon,

and IF YOU DARE!

ENTER
IF YOU DARE!

I spy

a cardinal,

 a lion's mane,

french fries,

 a 5,

and a yellow
airplane.

I spy

the ocean,

 a zebra,

a fan,

 two jars of paint,

and a pipe-cleaner man.

I spy

a battery,

 a faded blue N,

two thimbles,

 a guitar,

a spring,

 and a hen.

I spy

a horse,

 a red-and-white ball,

a musical note,

and a train that's small.

I spy

an arrowhead,

 a ring,

a key,

 a piece to a puzzle,

a trophy,

 and a G.

I spy

a soccer ball,

 a dog,

a bee,

 a green-and-yellow dress,

and a pot of tea.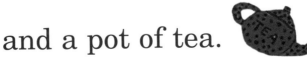

I spy

a ribbon,

a set of four,

a horse's wheels,

and a
GAME OF STORE.

I spy

a sword,

a phone,

a block T,

a trophy,

a magnet,

a duck,

and a wooden tree.

I spy

 a yellow car,

a playing-card tower,

 a lamb,

a phone,

 and a can of flour.

I spy two matching words.

yellow airplane

green-and-yellow dress

set of four

I spy two words that start
with the letter T.

two jars of paint

 can of flour

playing-card tower

I spy two matching words.

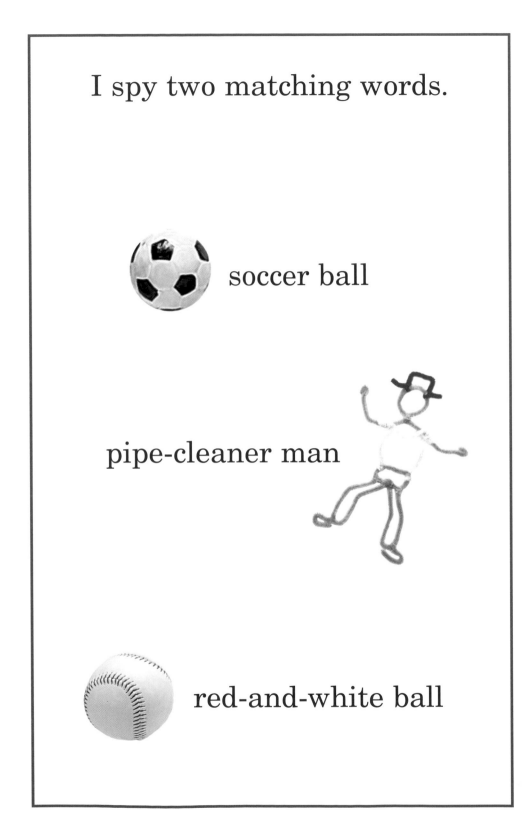

soccer ball

pipe-cleaner man

red-and-white ball

I spy two words that start with the letters TR.

lion's mane

wooden tree

 trophy

I spy two words that end with the letter Y.

battery

 thimbles

bushy hare

I spy two words that end with the letters LL.

soccer ball

 french fries

train that's small

I spy two words that rhyme.

key

musical note

pot of tea

I spy two words that rhyme.

 a hen

arrowhead

 blue N